It's Teatime, Winnie!

LAURA OWEN & KORKY PAUL

OXFORD
UNIVERSITY PRESS

Helping your child to read

Before they start

* Talk about the back cover blurb. How does your child think the bats might help Winnie when her bossy sister comes to tea?
* Look at the front cover. Does it give your child any clues about what might happen in the stories?

During reading

* Let your child read at their own pace – don't worry if it's slow. They could read silently, or read to you out loud.

* Help them to work out words they don't know by saying each sound out loud and then blending them to say the word, e.g. *s-au-ce, sauce.*
* If your child still struggles with a word, just tell them the word and move on.
* Give them lots of praise for good reading!

After reading

* Look at page 48 for some fun activities.

Contents

OXFORD
UNIVERSITY PRESS

Great Clarendon Street, Oxford OX2 6DP
Oxford University Press is a department of the University of Oxford.
It furthers the University's objective of excellence in research, scholarship,
and education by publishing worldwide. Oxford is a registered trade mark
of Oxford University Press in the UK and in certain other countries

"Winnie Goes Batty" was first published in *Winnie Goes Batty* 2010
"Winnie Grows Her Own" was first published in *Winnie Adds Magic* 2014
This edition published 2018

British Library Cataloguing in Publication Data

Data available

ISBN: 978-0-19-276521-5

3 5 7 9 10 8 6 4

OX27868901

Printed in China

Paper used in the production of this book is a natural,
recyclable product made from wood grown in sustainable forests.
The manufacturing process conforms to the environmental
regulations of the country of origin.

Acknowledgements
With thanks to Catherine Baker for editorial support

Winnie Goes Batty

⭑ Chapter ⭑ One

"Mmmm! Yummy in my tummy!" said Winnie, licking her fingers. She was sitting on the doorstep and eating turnip chips with snail sauce.

"Scrummy!" said Winnie, stuffing lots of chips into her mouth.

Then Winnie's bossy sister came round the corner.

"What is that rubbish you're eating,
Winnie?" she said, looking down her long
nose. "You should be eating good, fresh food
instead of fast food like this."

"How can you call snail sauce fast food?"
asked Winnie. "Anyway, I do cook fresh food
for Wilbur and for me."

"I'll come to tea later and see for myself,"
said her sister. "See you, then, Winnie.
Bye for now!"

9

Winnie hurried into the kitchen.

"Wilbur?" she called. "My sister is coming for tea, so we've got to cook up a feast. What shall we make?"

Wilbur looked in the fridge. "Meeow," he said. There was lots of squid.

"Good," said Winnie. "Squid in jelly for starters. Then for the main course we'll have batburgers. If there are lots of bats, we can make Battenberg cake, too!"

Wilbur opened the bat cupboard door. "Meeow!" said Wilbur, sadly.

"Knotted noodles, Wilbur!" said Winnie. "There's only one diddly little bat in there!"

"Squeak!" The diddly little bat looked at Winnie with its diddly batty eyes.

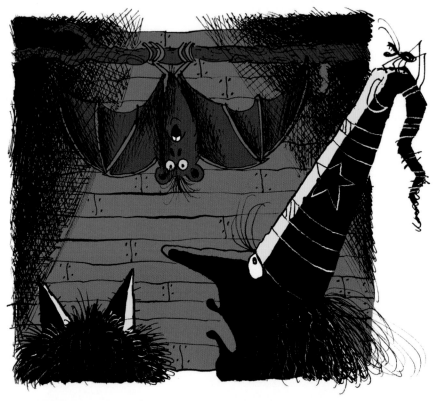

"Meeow?" asked Wilbur. He wanted to catch the diddly little bat.

"Stop, Wilbur!" said Winnie. "This bat's too teeny-tiny to cook. Let's go to the bat cave and get some big ones to mash into burgers."

⭐ Chapter ⭐
Two

Winnie and Wilbur flew off on the broom.

But Winnie couldn't sit still.

Jiggle-wriggle went the broom.
Swerve!

"Meeow!" said Wilbur, crossly.

"Sorry, Wilbur," said Winnie. "But
there's something itching and scratching
down my front."

Winnie pulled out something small and black from inside her dress. "Howling hats!" she said. "It's that diddly bat!"

The diddly bat trembled in her fingers. "Ah," said Winnie, suddenly going soppy. "It just wants to go home to the bat cave. Never mind, diddly bat! You can come with us," she said.

"Hmph!" said Wilbur. He wasn't going to get soppy over a bat.

They parked the broom outside the bat cave. Winnie found some nets for catching the bats.

"**Abracadabra!**" said Winnie to make her wand glow brightly.

Winnie and Wilbur could see bats clinging to all the walls. "Squeak! Squeak! Squeak!" went the bats.

"Pongy-wongy-woo!" said Winnie. "These bats smell lovely!"

Wilbur licked his lips. **Swish!** he went with his net.

Swish-swish! went Winnie's wand. "I've caught a bat!" she said.

The diddly bat climbed up Winnie's shoulder. "Squeak!"

"Oh!" said Winnie. "That bat is the diddly bat's mummy! He doesn't want her to be cooked in a burger."

So Winnie let the bat go.

Swish-swish-swat!

She caught another bat.

"This one is as fat as a flump dumpling!" said Winnie. Then Winnie noticed that it was rubbing its eyes. "Oh no! This fat bat's crying!"

"Squeak!" went the diddly bat.

"Flumping fishcakes!" said Winnie. "Is this fat bat your grandpa, diddly bat? It seems like every bat in the whole cave is part of your family!"

"Squeak!" went the diddly bat again. Winnie put down her net.

19

"Oh, I give up!" she said. "The diddly
bat's my friend, so I can't eat his family.
I shall make my sister a starter and that'll
have to do. Let's go, Wilbur!"

Winnie and Wilbur didn't spot the
diddly bat and his family following them
into the kitchen.

✯ Chapter ✯
Three

"Aha! Bottled flies," said Winnie. "Here's a packet of sun-dried lice, too. Get out the pans, Wilbur. Our guest will be here in five shakes of a cockroach's bottom."

Brriiiinnnnggg! Wiiiinnnniiiieeee! yelled the doorbell.

"Oh no! She's here already!" said Winnie.

Winnie opened the door, and there stood her sister. She had her enormous nose in the air, sniffing.

"What can you smell?" asked Winnie, a bit worried.

"Not a thing!" said her sister. "You haven't done any cooking, have you, Winnie? I just knew it!"

But just then, a sizzle sound came from the kitchen. A wonderful smell crept around the corner and up Winnie's sister's nose.

"Oh!" she said, as she stepped into the kitchen. "Wilbur is cooking, Winnie! Who's that helping him? Is it a bat?"

"It is," said Winnie. "That's my little diddly bat. And those other bats are his family!"

The bats were all helping Wilbur, stirring and chopping and fetching.

"What are we going to eat?" said Winnie's sister. "It does smell rather good!"

Winnie peeped into the pans. "Er … it's fly fritters with lice sprinkles."

"Very nice," said her sister.

And it was.

At last, Winnie's sister went home. The bats all hung themselves upside down in Winnie's room. Soon they were asleep.

"Night-night. Mind the cats don't bite," she said. She kissed the little diddly bat on the nose. "It looks fun to sleep upside down. I think I'll join you!"

Winnie hung herself from the curtain pole so that she could sleep like a bat, too. Wilbur slept upside down as well, until he fell off. *Flump!*

Winnie Grows Her Own

✦ Chapter One

"Home at last!" said Winnie, skipping up to her front door.

Winnie and Wilbur were just back from a holiday. It had rained all week. "That holiday was less fun than an itchy armpit," she said.

But now the sun was shining, and they were home.

"What shall we eat first, and second, and third?" asked Winnie. She turned the key and opened the door – **creak!** "Oh, yuck!" she said. The air in the house smelled stale and horrible.

"Meeow?" said Wilbur.

It was warmer and nicer outside the house than in it.

"Let's make a great big feast, and eat it outside to let some fresh air into the house," said Winnie.

Wilbur opened the fridge. It was empty except for a very disgusting smell. **Slam!** Wilbur shut the door fast.

Winnie opened the cupboard door. **Creak!**
Two bats and a beetle flew out. There was no
food inside.

"Oh, drat!" said Winnie. "We'll have to
go shopping."

So Winnie and Wilbur went to the shop,
but it was shut.

"Oh, double drat!" said Winnie. "Where
can we get some food?" Her tummy rumbled.

On the walk home, they passed fields of
cows and corn. They saw people carrying
bags of food for picnics.

"I know, Wilbur! We can grow our
own picnic!"

✫ Chapter Two

When they got back to their garden,
Winnie started work. "We need butter and
cheese," she said. She waved her wand once.
"**Abracadabra!**"

Suddenly, there was a cow. "**Moo!**"
Winnie waved her wand again.

"**Abracadabra!**" There were two woolly
goats. "**Berrr!**" said the goats.

"I want salad and crisps for the picnic," said Winnie. She pointed her wand, and made tomato and potato and cucumber plants. "And we need cake and bread!" Winnie waved her wand again. "**Abracadabra!**"

34

Suddenly, a flock of chickens appeared.

A patch of corn was growing around them.

Winnie looked around at her garden

farm. She took a deep breath of fresh air . . .

"Yuck!" said Winnie.

The cow and the goats and the chickens

had all done something very smelly.

"Quick, let's get working, Wilbur!" said
Winnie. "I'll cut the corn while you milk
the giddy goats. Soon we'll have bread and
pongy cheese for sandwiches."

Winnie bent over to cut the corn.

"**Berrr!**" said the goats, crossly. They didn't want to be milked. **Butt!** They charged into Winnie's bottom. **Wheee!** They flung her up in the air.

Splat! She landed on a great big cowpat. Winnie tried to get up, but she fell onto the corn and squashed it flat.

The chickens ran up to peck at the corn.

Peck! Peck!

The cow kicked over the bucket of milk, and trod on all the tomatoes and cucumbers.

Moo! Moo!

Suddenly Winnie's farm was a mess. Winnie was a mess. Wilbur was a mess.

"Bother!" said Winnie. She took off her muddy, stinky clothes. Then she waved her wand, "**Abracadabra!**" At once, her clothes were washed, and hanging up to dry.

"That's good!" said Winnie. "Now I need a bubble-scrubble bath to get me clean, too!"

★ Chapter ★ Three

Winnie's bubbly bath made her feel much better, but there was trouble when she went outside. A goat was eating her dress, the chickens were wearing her knickers and the cow was standing on her hat.

"Oh, frilly knickers!" cried poor Winnie. "I need my clothes! And my tummy is empty, and there's nothing to eat! It's not fair!"

Winnie stamped her foot crossly, and trod on an egg. **Crack-splat!**

"Now I can't even have an egg to eat!" said Winnie.

She closed her eyes. Wilbur was worried — he thought Winnie was going to cry. So he came up with a clever plan.

He whizzed round the garden and got some wool from the goats. **Clickety-click!** He quickly knitted the wool into a hairy brown costume for Winnie. He stuck chicken feathers all over it.

"Oooh, thank you, Wilbur!" said Winnie, putting the costume on. "That's as cosy as a hug from a bug in a rug!"

Winnie looked like a Winniebeast now!

Wilbur wrote a big sign …

He made the Winniebeast stand behind the sign.

Some people were walking past, carrying food for a picnic. They stopped and stared. Then they gave the Winniebeast some of their cakes and sandwiches and drinks.

"**Cock-a-doodle-moo!**" said the strange Winniebeast, thanking them.

She gave some of the food to Wilbur. All afternoon, Winnie and Wilbur ate cakes and sandwiches and pies and biscuits.

"**Cock-a-doodle-moo!**" said Winnie happily, to the last person who gave her a bit of picnic.

When it got dark, the picnickers went home, and so did Winnie and Wilbur. The house smelled much nicer now.

"Do you know what, Wilbur?" said Winnie. "I'm glad there's no food in the house, because I won't be hungry again for at least a week!"

The costume was so nice and cosy that Winnie didn't even need to change into her nightie for bed. And Wilbur had a lovely, soft, warm sleep on the hairy Winniebeast.

After reading activities

Quick quiz

See how fast you can answer these questions!
Look back at the stories if you can't
remember.

1) In "Winnie Goes Batty", why doesn't
   Winnie want to eat the bats after all?
2) In "Winnie Grows Her Own", what is the
   Winniebeast?
3) In "Winnie Grows Her Own", how
   do Winnie and Wilbur get food for
   their picnic?

1) they are all related to her friend, the little diddly bat. 2) Winnie
wearing a hairy brown costume. 3) passers-by give it to them.

Talk about it!

★ What would you give to Winnie to eat,
  if she came round to your house for tea?
  Write and draw a menu for her. You
  could add lots of witchy treats like
  slug squash, caterpillar cupcakes and
  creepy crawlies!